A book about giving and receiving....

by Holly Roberts Merrell

What Would You Do With A Million Dollars?

Illustrations by Galih Winduadi

Library of Congress Control Number: 2020902180

ISBN: 978-1-951982-00-3
Digital ISBN: 978-1-951982-01-0

What are your thoughts about money?

Many of us were taught that money is bad. Many people misunderstand the verse in the bible that says..."the love of money is the root of all evil." "Money" and "the love of money" are two entirely different things. Money is simply a "tool". We can use this tool for good or bad, right or wrong.

Take a hammer for instance. Who's to say that a hammer is bad? It can do a lot of good and help people in many ways. But if used the wrong way, it can do a lot of harm and damage. Money is the same way. We can use it for evil, or we can use it to do good and help not only ourselves, but others. The person holding it gets to decide which way they choose to use it.

Did you know that some of the most wealthy people in this world are givers? They give and give and give! If you were to study their lives, you would see how generous they really are. They understand the law of the universe that states... "When we give, something always comes back." This is one of the main reasons they are so wealthy.

Many of us have this backwards. We say to ourselves... "Once I receive, then I will give." We may feel that we don't have anything to give, but this is not true. At the moment, it may not be money that we can give, but we all have something to share.

We are here to help each other out, and as we do, we are always blessed in return. As you read through this story, feel free to dream. Dream about all the different things you would do with a million bucks. And think of all the ways you could share it to bless the lives of others.

WHAT WOULD YOU DO WITH A MILLION DOLLARS?

$1,000,000

Would you buy a sports car?
Would you buy some trucks?
Or would you buy a tractor
with those million bucks?

Would you buy a cabin?
Would you buy a home?
Would you travel to London?
Would you travel to Rome?

Would you go on a cruise,
or go camping in the trees?
Would you buy a tent,
or would you buy some skis?

Would you buy a horse?
Would you buy a cow?
Does it snow where you live,
and you need a snowplow?

Would you buy a snowmobile,
or would you buy a boat?
Would you buy a swimsuit,
or would you buy a coat?

Would you share what you have
and give to the needy?
Or keep it all yourself
and choose to be greedy?

It's great to want things,
that's how it should be.
And when you give to others,
you actually receive.

You may not notice,
at least not right away,
but what you give out
will come back in some way.

It's not always money
that you will receive.
It might be something you've worked at
that you finally achieve.

It might come unexpected.
It might come right away.
It might take a year.
It might take a day.

It might come as a feeling.
It might come as love.
It might come from a neighbor.
It might come from above.

But whenever you give,
something always comes back.
And you'll find that you're blessed,
you will seldom lack.

The more that you give,
the more you'll receive.
You just have to give,
then have faith and believe.

Sometimes it's hard
to give what you have.
But one day you'll find out,
it's not really that bad.

You'll see more blessings
coming your way,
and your life will improve
more and more everyday!

So you can choose to be selfish,
and keep it for your own.
But one day you can't say,
"I wish I'd have known."

Because I'm telling you this,
and I'm teaching you now,
when you give, you receive,
and blessings you allow.

So if I ask this question
to you just one more time,
consider what I told you,
and get rid of mine, mine, mine.

What would you do with a million dollars?

Would you buy some golf clubs?
Would you buy a guitar?
And then help your neighbor
with his broken down car?

Would you go on vacation
and have some fun?
And then do some service
when you are done?

Would you go scuba diving?
Would you go on a cruise?
And would you give some money
to a kid with no shoes?

Would you go out to eat
and have a kebab?
And take along a family
whose dad lost his job?

Would you go to Disneyland
and buy a day pass?
And on your way home
help a gal with no gas?

Would you fly to Hawaii
and spend a week in the sun?
Then do Sub-For-Santa
for a family who has none?

Money's not evil,
it's very good;
as long as we do
the things that we should.

We can have for ourselves,
but we can also give.
This is the way
that we should live.

So as you are blessed
and have things you can share,
whether your time, or your talents,
or even a prayer,

your life will get better
and you'll see a change.
At first you may think
this "giving" is strange.

But as you see the blessings
that start coming in,
you'll see I'm not lying,
when we give....we WIN!

WHAT WOULD YOU DO WITH A MILLION DOLLARS?

Books by Holly Roberts Merrell...

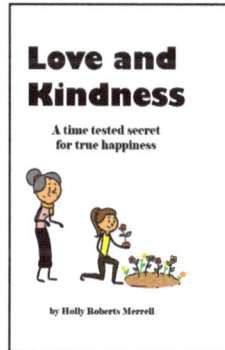

What would YOU do with a Million Dollars?

A book about giving and receiving...
By Holly Roberts Merrell

A book for all ages...

Get Back Up and Keep on Trying

by Holly Roberts Merrell

The Power of...
"I AM"

by Holly Roberts Merrell

The Healing Power of Forgiveness

I forgive
I forgive
I forgive

by Holly Roberts Merrell

Love and Kindness

A time tested secret for true happiness

by Holly Roberts Merrell

To learn more about the author and more in depth detail of her personal experiences regarding her books, please visit hollyrobertsmerrell.com.

www.ingramcontent.com/pod-product-compliance
Lightning Source LLC
Chambersburg PA
CBHW041818040426
42452CB00001B/17